B.I.L.Y. (Because I Love You)

Love
Bites

A Cookbook For
Romantic Encounters

By Culinary Advisor & Celebrity Master Chef
Jacques Prudhomme

Temple Publishing LLC
Cleveland, OH

Legacy Imprint of
TEMPLE PUBLISHING GROUP LLC
Cleveland, Ohio USA
www.templepublishing.com

First Edition

Print History
First Printing, January 2000

Printed in the United States of America

10 9 8 7 6 5 4 3 2 1

ISBN No. 1-58446-001-6

Culinary Editorial Staff
Master Chef Jacques Prudhomme
Bobby Fairman
Alex Procaccini

Wine Editorial Staff
Robin Woodbury, Woodbury Vineyards

Text & Cover Design
Doreen M. Buck

Prudhomme

Dear Reader,

Through the sands of time, the orchard of the Garden of Eden has expanded into a progressive variety of thousands of Love Bites, which we describe in modern terms as hors d'oeuvres, canapés, appetizers, etc.

Since pre-historic civilizations, the interpretation of Love Bite has evolved from a couple of ribs of dinosaurs to more delicate feasts; the meaning, however, remains the same. Food in any form or presentation plays a key role in romantic encounters and always will.

Think about it for a minute! How would you feel trying to make love with a full stomach? Would this be uncomfortable? But of course!

Certain foods can have a mysterious effect, both physical and mental, in exciting the appetite. The history of mankind illustrates through, a multitude of manuscripts and motion pictures, that Love Bites, as we describe here, are, and have played, a major role in the union of love. Later, Love Bites were complemented with a variety of nectars of the gods which we call wines. Good wine and food are the perfect match for a Love Bite Encounter.

We all know that romantic urges have no pre-set time therefore this book should always be kept on hand. You never know when an opportunity will present itself. It could be mid-morning, afternoon, evening or even in the early hours before the morning after.

Wines, cheeses, fruits, and breads should always be part of your Love Bites reserve. There are thousands of easy to prepare recipes. Even if you are not an expert in cooking, you can create a romantic Love Bite. Just follow the easy step-by-step instructions in my book.

This book has been designed for both sexes. It can apply to a lover, a new flame or your loving spouse. Many of us have the habit of taking love for granted which can be devastating. There is something very special about the setting for romantic encounters so we have included some hints about where to conduct your Love Bites, as well as ways to help create an appropriate mood.

Is it important to have a Love Bite encounter? We will present a fully researched scenario for you and you be the judge.

Let's imagine it is about 10:00 PM and you just finished watching a movie on television with that special person. You are wondering what to do next. Answer, slip away to the kitchen and pick up the Love Bites cookbook. Select one of the thirty-five selections that take just a few moments to prepare. Walk back to the living room; put soft music on and light some candles. Dim the lights to create a romantic atmosphere. Sitting on the floor by the coffee table, open a bottle of wine. As love pours from your eyes in the direction of your companion, fill the wineglasses and propose a toast to the beginning of a perfect evening.

After a few moments slip back into the kitchen and bring out the appetizers. Follow this with romantic compliments to your partner. Don't you think for a minute that the excitement will take place just in you your mind and heart!

The coffee table is just one place to begin the eventful evening. It could be in the bedroom, the patio or any other place of convenience. Again, remember Love Bites have a very mystical way of creating a passionate urge.

In this special book, you have many choices of ingredients, which can be stimulating and will excite your love appetite. Many can provide energy and we know how important that is. The advantage of Love Bites is it only takes a few bites to produce the special effect you are hoping for. You mustn't worry about your diet. We promise the calories will burn up fast.

Love Bites can also be rewarding *after* a romantic encounter where you have used up a lot of energy. Who knows, when recharged, you may have the urge for a rematch…why not? Remember that there are no set rules.

It is important to have an ample supply of assorted foods for Love Bite Encounters. You will find ideas in this book to suit many occasions, so *bon appetit!*

Let "*B.I.L.Y. (Because I Love You) Love Bites*" cookbook be your secret romance weapon. It won't be the same, believe us! Romantic encounters without Love Bites is like a meal without wine. At least it's the way of fifty million French people.

Romance and passion are very important in our life. Besides solidifying a relationship, it also relieves tension and with the help of the "*B.I.L.Y. Love Bites*" cookbook, the guesswork is eliminated.

Now that you are convinced of how important the "*B.I.L.Y. Love Bites*" cookbook can be for you, let us show you how simple it is to prepare some exciting encounters.

First, read all the different recipes appropriate to the different moods and settings. Read the shopping list and the Love Bites pantry list. You should keep some of these items on hand for unexpected opportunities. If single, you never know when an old flame or a new flame may show up. If you are married, any time is the right time to rekindle the flame that burned many years before so being ready is being one step ahead.

All of the Love Bites in this cookbook are very easy to prepare. Just follow step-by-step, the techniques, hints and preparation instructions and *voila!*...You are on your way to success in the romance department

It is important to keep focused on romance with every bite. Food alone will not do, so try some of the ideas we present for creating a romantic mood. Better yet, think of some of your own, especially for your special partner.

There is only one cardinal rule with Love Bites. Garlic or onions are NEVER included in a Love Bite. Other than that, let your romantic imagination go to work for you.

I wish to offer this Love Bite toast … "May you be bitten by B.I.L.Y. Love Bites forever!"

Jacques Prudhomme

TABLE OF CONTENTS · PAGE NO.

LOVE BITES · PAGE NO.

Love Bites By Setting & Food Type

Love Bite by Menu Item

Menu Item	Love Bite Number

SEAFOOD (CONTINUED)

- Clam 23
- Crabmeat 35
- Crawfish Tails 33
- Lobster Tail 25
- Mussels 2
- Oysters 3,18,21,28,34
- Scallops 6
- Shrimp 1,14,32

MISCELLANEOUS

- Artichoke Hearts 5
- Caviar 13
- Crepes 10
- Hearts of Palm 25
- Spinach 34
- Zucchini 30

NECTAR OF THE GODS

(Wine, Champagne & Spirits)
Suggested Woodbury Wines and
Champagnes are listed. Substitute as
necessary.

Item	Love Bite Number

- Seaport White 1,14
- Dry Riesling 2,10,24,35
- Brut Champagne 3,18,24
- Glacier Ridge Red 4,15
- Seyval 5,16
- Chardonnay 6,13,23,28,32,33
- Riesling Champagne 7
- Seaport Blush 8,22,31
- Chautauqua Champagne 9
- Seaport Red 11,30
- Tequila 12
- Red Renard 17
- Merlot 19
- Barrel Fermented Chardonnay ...
  20,21
- French Pernod® 25
- Imperial Sake 26,27
- White Renard 29

ACCESSORY SHOPPING LIST

Candles

Be sure to have a variety of sizes,
shapes and styles of candles on hand.
Long tapers for elegance, votive
candles for spiritual effect and lantern candles for practicality and long
life. Candles can be scented or un-
scented.

Aromatherapy

Essential oils and Aromatherapy
products can be used alone, or a few
drops added to the candle will create
a romantic fragrance to heighten the
senses. Following is a partial list of
scents for various moods.

- Tropical Island—Patchouli,
    Ylang-Ylang
- Adventure—Bergamot
- Elegance—Amber
- Serenity—Rose
- Innocence—Lilac or Violet
- Night Life—Jasmine
- Spring—Lavender
- Light & Delightful—Cinnamon
- Intrigue—Musk
- Freshness—Sandalwood

Fresh Flowers

From the simple elegant daisy to the
complex elegant rose, fresh flowers are
a symbol of love and beauty. Following are fragrant flowers and some
possible uses of specific flowers.

- Sweet Pea—Pure perfume odor
- Stocks—Spicy
- Peony—Sweet buttery
- Freesia—Sweet smelling
- Carnation—Clove-like
- Aloha Rose—Fruity
- Regal Lilies—Warm, spicy

ACCESSORIES (FLOWERS CONTINUED)

- Phlox—Tangy
- Snapdragons—Fresh grass
- Honeysuckle—Nutmeg
- Roses—Sweet, fruity, musk
- Marigolds—Sharp, tangy
- Lilacs—Sweet
- Geranium—Tart, lemony

Pink carnations are very romantic – known for carrying the message "always lovely." Roses, of course, are the symbol of love.

Music

A myriad of musical backgrounds can enhance the Love Bite Encounter. You should make sure you have music with instrumentals, as well as vocals, for your music library. Remember the music should not be competing with you during your romantic conversation.

Keep on hand, music that is romantic and mood setting. Nature's sounds, soulful jazz, uplifting new age, classical or string quartets or ethnic ballads will put you and your partner in the mood for a B.I.L.Y. Love Bite. The more varied your collection, the more opportunities you will have to be adventuresome.

One of the latest innovations is the Zenith Soothing Sounds and Aroma Therapy Alarm Clock Radio. It might come in handy as you set the mood for your love bites. For more information visit website at www.sdidirect.com.

Love Bite Pantry Shopping List:

Prepare a special area in your kitchen cupboard to store items you may need for an impromptu Love Bite. The following is a list of items you might not normally have:

- Artichoke hearts
- Bakers Chocolate (semi-sweet)
- Corn syrup
- Capers (small)
- Caviar (black and red)
- Crackers (Melba Toast, saltine, wheat crackers, whole grain)
- Clam juice
- Chicken broth
- Cocktail sauce
- Coconut cream
- Curry Paste (yellow)
- Dijon mustard
- Hearts of Palm
- Honey
- Horseradish sauce
- Lemon Juice
- Lime Juice
- Marmalade
- Mushrooms (canned)
- Olives (black)
- Olive oil
- Oysters (Canned)
- Pate de foie gras au truffles
- Peanut butter
- Peanut oil
- Pickles (sweet, sour)
- Pineapple rings (canned)
- Raspberry preserves
- Salsa
- Swiss white chocolate

As needed, pick up the following fresh items:

Fresh Vegetables
- Bell Pepper (red, green, yellow, jalapeño)
- Cabbage (red)
- Celery
- Lettuce (bib, endive, romaine)
- Mushrooms
- Spinach
- Zucchini

Fresh Fruits
- Apple (Delicious)
- Avocado
- Banana
- Grapes (red, green, purple)
- Lemon
- Lime
- Mango
- Pear
- Starfruit
- Strawberries

Dairy
- Butter
- Cheese (Brie, Cheddar, Cream cheese, Jalapeño, Jack, Mozzarella, Romano, Roquefort, and Swiss)
- Eggs
- Milk
- Whipping Cream

Love Bite Spice Cupboard:
There is a special treat in the Love Bite Spice Cupboard. Master Chef Jacques Prudhomme has created a set of special spices called Aromantic Seasonings of Seduction. They have been prepared in regular and spicy strength. These special blended spices can be found in selected grocery and gourmet stores. If they are not available in your area, you may substitute Old Bay® Seasoning. The seasonings are guaranteed to enhance the flavor of the food and produce a seductive aroma from the kitchen to help you complete the B.I.L.Y. Love Bite mood.

Check your cupboard to make sure you have these other spices on hand:
- Allspice
- Anise
- Basil
- Bay leaf
- Cloves (ground)
- Cornstarch
- Cumin
- Dill
- Ginger Powder
- Mustard (dry)
- Nutmeg
- Paprika
- Pepper (black crushed, cayenne)
- Rosemary
- Salt (rock, table)
- Savory

Try to have the following fresh herbs on hand:
- Basil
- Cilantro
- Parsley

The following sauces will be useful:
- Soy sauce
- Tabasco sauce
- Worcestershire sauce

A "Love Notes" page at the end of each Love Bite will allow you to make notes for future Love Bites. Perhaps you will just want to create a written record of its success.

Woodbury Vineyards, Inc. e-mail: wv@woodburyvineyards.com
3230 S. Roberts Road Web Page: www.woodburyvineyards.com
Fredonia, NY 14063 Toll Free: (888) NYS-WINE

Master Chef Jacques Prudhomme is proud to be the official culinary advisor to Woodbury Vineyards and heartily endorses their award winning palate of exceptionally fine wines.

⧉ The tradition of winemaking at Woodbury Vineyards ⧉

Woodbury Vineyards is located in Western New York's Chautauqua County, the third largest grape-growing region in America. The Woodbury family has been tilling the soil near the Village of Fredonia since 1910. The winery was added to the business in 1979. Today Woodbury wines are regularly recognized for outstanding quality in national and international competitions.

Woodbury Vineyards is nestled in the shadow of the escarpment separating the Lake Erie plain from the forested foothills of the Allegheny mountains. The rich porous soil of the glacial ridges allows the vine roots to penetrate 20-30 feet. Large and shallow Lake Erie cools the area in the summer and warms it in the winter moderating temperature extremes. This unique soil and climate yields grapes with significant aromas, a ripe sugar/acid balance and full maturity.

Woodbury Vineyards wines have earned an impressive number of awards and medals in national and international competitions including best Northern Hemisphere Chardonnay.

The winery is open daily for tours, tasting and sales. Visit the website www.woodburyvineyards.com for more information and list of scheduled events including those featuring Master Chef Jacques Prudhomme.

Love Bite No. 1
(Love Me Tenderly)

SETTING

The setting for this Love Bite takes place at a coffee table in the living room.

CREATE THE MOOD

First, in a charming voice, ask your companion if you could be excused for a few minutes because you have a little surprise.

Dim the lights and light the candles, turn on the CD or tape for soft romantic music and open a bottle of wine or champagne. Pour a glass for each of you and make a toast by saying that you feel very romantic tonight and that patience will be rewarded. Then, go to the kitchen and begin preparations of your selected Love Bite.

LOVE BITE MENU

- Champignons de Crevette
  (Mushroom caps stuffed with shrimp)

JACQUES RECOMMENDS

Woodbury's Seaport White, a blend of Seyval and Cayuga. Flavorful and well-balanced, this selection will blend well with this Love Bite.

INGREDIENTS

*If Aromantic Seasonings of Seduction is not available in your area, you may use Old Bay® Seasoning.

6 large mushroom caps
8 oz. of fresh shrimp peeled and deveined
¼ cup mayonnaise
¼ cup cream cheese
¼ cup grated Swiss cheese
2 tablespoons bread crumbs
1/8 teaspoon of Spicy Aromantic Seasonings of
    Seduction*
1/8 teaspoon of nutmeg
Pinch of salt and paprika
2 quarts of boiling water with 1 tablespoon salt

PREPARATION

Set oven temperature at 400°. Remove stems from mushroom caps and clean caps with a paper tissue. Place caps in a casserole. In a large pot bring water and salt to boiling point, add shrimp, and cook 3 minutes. Drain water quickly and rinse in cold running water for 1 minute. Drain thoroughly. In a mixing bowl stir mayonnaise, cream cheese, one half of Swiss cheese, spices and salt. Mix thoroughly with a spoon or whisk until creamy. Cut each shrimp into 3 pieces and add to bowl. Mix thoroughly. Fill mushroom caps with mixture. Mix together and then sprinkle the remaining 1/2 of Swiss cheese and breadcrumbs with paprika on the filled mushroom caps. Bake in oven for 15 minutes and serve.

PREPARATION TIME

30 Minutes

PRESENTATION

Place mushroom caps on a serving platter, which you have lined with lettuce leaves. You may add some black olives and lemon wedges for decoration. French bread can be served, if you wish.

 MASTER CHEF COMMENTS

You will be delighted with this Love Bite. Should you look forward to the next one?

But of course!

_____

_____

_____

_____

_____

_____

_____

_____

_____

_____

_____

_____

Love Bite No. 2
(Blue Moon in the Night)

SETTING

The setting for this Love Bite is a moonlit evening on the patio or sunny afternoon in the garden. There is no better setting than moonlight however, a warm breezy sunny day can also be very romantic.

CREATE THE MOOD

If in the moonlight, light candles. In the background soft romantic music must be playing in order for the Love Bite to be more effective. Of course, a nice chilled bottle of white wine is also in order. On the table place several votive candles. After lighting them and pouring a glass of wine for your partner, quietly excuse yourself.

LOVE BITE MENU

- Moules Almandine Cilantro
  (Baked mussels with almonds and cilantro)

JACQUES RECOMMENDS

Woodbury's Dry Riesling, is an excellent vintage. In the Alsatian style this fine wine, with hints of melon and a floral bouquet is excellent with this Love Bite.

INGREDIENTS

*If Aromantic Seasonings of Seduction is not available in your area, you may use Old Bay® Seasoning.

24 fresh mussels
¼ cup of ground almonds
¼ cup olive oil
2 tablespoons of lemon juice
1/8 teaspoon of Regular Aromantic Seasonings of Seduction*
¼ cup of chopped fresh cilantro
4 dashes of Tabasco® sauce
4 dashes of Worcestershire sauce
¼ teaspoon salt
4 slices of toasted French or Italian bread.

PREPARATION

Heat oven to 450°. Scrub and wash mussels. In a large pot add one quart of water and bring to a boil. Add mussels, cover and cook on high heat for a few minutes. Keep watching closely and as soon as mussels open, drain. Remove and discard part of the shell. Place each mussel on baking tray. Mix all other ingredients together and spoon evenly on top of each mussel. Bake for 10 to 15 minutes. Remove from oven as soon as they are bubbling. Serve with toasted bread.

PREPARATION TIME

35 Minutes

PRESENTATION

Shred several leaves of lettuce and cover dinner plate. Place 12 mussels on each plate. Cut a lemon in half and place a little bouquet of parsley in the center.

MASTER CHEF COMMENTS

Will this Love Bite be a sure-fire success?

But of course!

_____

_____

_____

_____

_____

_____

_____

_____

_____

_____

_____

Love Bite No. 3
(Tonight My Love)

SETTING

This advanced setting takes place in the bedroom, right on top of your king or queen size bed. Don't worry about breadcrumbs. It won't be on the menu.

CREATE THE MOOD

A Love Bite in your bedroom can be very romantic and the advantage is you are right in the Love Nest. How convenient can it be? We only suggest this bedroom scenario IF the couple involved agree a lovemaking session may be involved. Perhaps we should also mention that not all love bite romances end up in love making at first. It may take a couple Love Bites for someone new to respond and agree. If either party is uncertain then it may be better to try the patio or living room for the setting. Caution is advised though because the ingredients in this menu act like an aphrodisiac. Oysters have their special ways of communicating.

LOVE BITE MENU

- Oysters Valentino

JACQUES RECOMMENDS

1 Bottle of Brut Champagne or Chardonnay from Woodbury will make this Love Bite even more exciting than it already is.

INGREDIENTS

24 blue point oysters, raw in shells.
1 large red bell pepper
1 lemon
6 small Jalapeño peppers
¼ cup olive oil
1/8 cup lime juice
¼ cup chopped parsley
¼ cup bread crumbs
¼ cup Romano grated cheese
1 package of your favorite crackers or Melba toast
Rock salt

PREPARATION

What we said about crumbs in bed…well we lied, but who cares. It's worth it! Set oven at broil. First, scrub and wash oysters thoroughly. Using a towel and an oyster knife, you can pry open oysters easily. Remove top lid and discard. Loosen attached membrane of oyster. Line baking tray with rock salt and place oysters on top. Wash red bell pepper and Jalapeño peppers. Wipe dry and rub with a little olive oil. Place them on a cookie sheet. Increase oven to broil and place tray under the broiler. Broil peppers on all sides. When skin breaks, remove and let cool. Reduce oven temperature to 450º. Peel bell pepper and Jalapeño peppers; remove inside and dice finely.

NOTE: Seeds from the Jalapeño pepper are very hot so do not use your fingers to remove the seeds as the effect of them will remain on your fingers. Use a knife or a paper towel.

Mix olive oil, lime juice, chopped parsley, peppers, breadcrumbs and grated Romano cheese together. Spread equally on top of each oyster. Bake for 8 to 10 minutes or until light brown and serve.

PREPARATION TIME

30 Minutes

PRESENTATION

Shred lettuce to cover large dinner plate. Arrange oysters around plate leaving center for lemon wedges. If you don't have a bed tray to put plate on, don't worry, use two cookie sheets instead. Place a half-folded tablecloth over tray to stabilize plates, leaving room for the candle and side plate. By sitting Indian style you can face each other and exchange romantic words and sip the wine. At the end of your Love Bite when romance is at its hottest, just move the candle and wine glass, pick up the four corners of the tablecloth, bundle up the service pieces and place it on the floor.

 MASTER CHEF COMMENTS

Don't let yourself cool off for a second, right?

But of course!

_____

_____

_____

_____

_____

_____

_____

_____

_____

_____

_____

Love Bite No. 4
(Country Love)

SETTING

The setting for this Love Bite romance is perfect for a country location, like on a farm. Just think how romantic it would be to have this Love Bite in a barn on top of a haystack. All you have to worry about is not to start a fire with the candles. This Love Bite is designed to bring your bodies to a very high temperature, but don't worry, it won't start a fire.

CREATE THE MOOD

The atmosphere of the setting will create the mood you are looking for. If you have a portable CD or cassette player, you may want to play soft romantic background music also.

LOVE BITE MENU

- French Style Picnic à la Campagne

Jacques Recommends

1 bottle of Woodbury's Glacier Ridge Red is the perfect compliment to this Love Bite. It is a dry red wine blend of Ruby Cabernet, Cabernet Franc and Merlot.

Ingredients

1 French baguette bread
1 – 6 oz. jar of Dijon mustard
¼ lb. Brie cheese
¼ lb. Pate de foie gras au truffles
1 Delicious apple
1 pear

Preparation & Presentation

This one will require your expertise in shopping for the following:

- Picnic basket,
- Tablecloth (red and white squares) with matching napkins.
- Wine bottle opener
- Small bread knife or serrated steak knife
- Fat candle, like a lantern candle, for safety.
- Blanket
- Portable CD or audio cassette player
- Twine

Voila! All you have to do is drive to the country to find a farm if you do not have one. If a farmer agrees to let you use their barn, which should not be too difficult, the only thing you may have to worry about is the fact you may be the highlight of the village for quite some time.

NOTE: Use the twine to tie together straw, clover or wheat (or other natural item you can find) for decoration for your place setting.

 Master Chef Comments

Spontaneity is one of the best ingredients of romance. Ask yourself, "Would I do anything for a different Love Bite romance?"

But of course!

_____

_____

_____

_____

_____

_____

_____

_____

_____

_____

_____

_____

Love Bite No. 5
(In The Mood For Love)

SETTING

Choose any place that is comfortable for you and your partner.

CREATE THE MOOD

Most Love Bites are popular seafood items, however, a lot of Love Bites have been successful with different food like poultry, beef, pork, fish, veal or wild game. Love Bites come in many different flavors however, the basic mood-setters remain the same. A nice table with candles, roses, wineglasses, soft romantic music and above all, a seductive companion. As for wine, it is a matter of personal choice but Woodbury has a wonderful selection to choose from.

LOVE BITE MENU

- Fond D'artichaut De Poulet
  (Artichoke hearts stuffed with chicken)

Jacques Recommends

Woodbury's Seyval, chilled will create yet another memory of this Love Bite. It is a light, aromatic and easy to drink wine.

Ingredients

*If Aromantic Seasonings of Seduction is not available in your area, you may use Old Bay® Seasoning.

1 can of artichokes hearts
    (contains 6 hearts per can)
8 oz. chicken breast or 2 small single breasts
1 tablespoon of butter
1 tablespoon of flour
½ cup of milk
1 tablespoon of oil
4 ounces of grated Swiss cheese
1 teaspoon of Regular Aromantic
    Seasonings of Seduction*
Pinch of dry mustard
Dash of salt and pepper
Paprika
1 tomato
Parsley

Preparation

Set oven to 400°. Drain artichoke hearts. Rub chicken breasts with oil and sprinkle with salt & pepper and place in an oven-proof dish. Bake for 15 to 18 minutes. Set aside to cool. In a saucepan melt butter slowly, add flour and stir with whisk until flour is absorbed in butter. Add milk, stirring constantly until a thick consistency is reached.

Cook for 2 minutes. Remove from burner and add spices. Dice chicken breasts and add to mixture. Add cheese and stir. Fill middle of artichoke hearts with mixture to form a dome. Sprinkle with paprika. Bake for 12 to 15 minutes.

PREPARATION TIME

35 Minutes

PRESENTATION

Slice tomato and arrange on a bed of lettuce. Place 3 hearts on each dinner plate. Sprinkle with salt and pepper and serve.

 MASTER CHEF COMMENTS

Will your companion be impressed with this Love Bite?

But of course!

_____

_____

_____

_____

_____

_____

_____

_____

_____

_____

_____

_____

Love Bite No. 6
(Love Me Always)

SETTING

The setting for this Love Bite romance can be in the dining room.

CREATE THE MOOD

A dozen roses, candlelight and soft romantic music. Using the dining room doesn't mean it has to be formal. You could even be in your robe if it is for a special occasion, like getting your companion in a semi-formal mood, or just to be different.

LOVE BITE MENU

- Coquille St. Jacques III
  (Sautéed scallops in white wine sauce)

Jacques Recommends

1 chilled bottle of Woodbury Chardonnay should heat up this Love Bite.

Ingredients

*If Aromantic Seasonings of Seduction is not available in your area, you may use Old Bay® Seasoning.

6 pieces of large deep sea scallops
½ cup of fresh cream
¼ cup white wine
2 tablespoons of butter
2 egg yolks
1/8 teaspoon dry mustard
¼ teaspoon Regular Aromantic Seasonings of
    Seduction*
Pinch salt and pepper
1 lemon sliced
1 tablespoon parsley
2 slices of French bread

Preparation

Wash and clean membranes of scallops and sponge dry. Cut them in half and roll them in flour. Shake off excess flour. In a large frying pan over medium fire, melt butter and add scallops. Cook 5 to 8 minutes, turning on all sides. Remove from pan, set aside. Add white wine to the pan and reduce liquid by 2/3. Add half the cream and cook until mixture thickens. Beat egg yolks with the other half of cream, add to pan stirring constantly. Add spices when thickening and reduce fire to low. Add scallops and cook slowly for 2 to 3 minutes.

PREPARATION TIME

20 Minutes

PRESENTATION

Divide scallops and sauce into 2 serving casserole
dishes, if you have them, or salad plates will do.
Chop parsley and sprinkle over scallops. Cut slice
of lemon as decoration. Serve with one slice of
French bread, which is perfect to dip in sauce
with each Love Bite.

 MASTER CHEF COMMENTS

Will the amazing results of this Love Bite
romance continue long after the event?

But of course!

_____

_____

_____

_____

_____

_____

_____

_____

_____

_____

_____

_____

_____

Love Bite No. 7
(The More The Better)

SETTING

The scenario for this Love Bite Romance is a little on the wild side if you feel it is appropriate. Let's do things in reverse for a change. Let's say earlier in the evening you could not restrain the urge of lovemaking and it is only 10:00 PM on a Saturday Night. What do you do for an encore?

CREATE THE MOOD

Well it is easy. Ask your mate to prepare the hot tub or Jacuzzi while you go to the kitchen and prepare Love Bites. Give your companion five or six candles to place around the tub and of course play romantic background music. On your return, you can begin your Love Bite romance in the tub.

LOVE BITE MENU

- Fruits Au Chocolat
  (Assorted fresh fruits dipped in dark chocolate)

JACQUES RECOMMENDS

Bring out a nice bottle of Woodbury chilled Riesling Champagne to make this Love Bite special. The rich Riesling fruit is balanced with lots of bubbles!

INGREDIENTS

8 large strawberries
1 ripe pear
1 red delicious apple
Approximately 20 seedless grapes
1 package (12 oz.) of dark semi-sweet baker chocolate
1 tablespoon of corn syrup
2 oz. lemon juice

PREPARATION

In a double boiler melt chocolate, stirring often. Add corn syrup, stir and keep warm. Fruit should be refrigerated at least 2 hours before preparation. Wash grapes, strawberries and pat dry. Peel and core pear and apple and slice into 8 quarters. Soak apple and pear quarters in lemon juice for five minutes and pat dry. Use a cookie sheet or pan and line with wax paper. Use heavy round toothpicks to insert into fruit and then dip the fruit halfway into chocolate. Lay them on the cookie sheet pan for 10 minutes or so.

NOTE: This Love Bite can be made ahead of time and kept refrigerated until ready to serve.

PREPARATION TIME

20 Minutes

PRESENTATION

If you have a nice silver tray, it is best but, if not, use a large flat platter. You may cut the rose from its stem and place it in the middle of the tray for decoration. If not, a small bouquet of parsley will do also.

 MASTER CHEF COMMENTS

This Love Bite romance may just bring on an encore. Should you stay in the tub while enjoying this Love Bite?

But of course!

_____

_____

_____

_____

_____

_____

_____

_____

_____

_____

_____

_____

Love Bite No. 8
(Under The Tree)

SETTING

The setting for this Love Bite should be impromptu and in a public place, like for instance, a public park.

CREATE THE MOOD

The charm of this Love Bite is the fact that it is being conducted on a beautiful day, on the grass in a park. It can be very sentimental. Bring along a portable CD or audio cassette player and classical music. Mozart, would be perfect for this setting.

LOVE BITE MENU

- Canapés au Jambon et Caprés
- Canapés Roule à la Dinde
  (Mini-sandwiches with ham and capers and Rolled turkey sandwiches)

JACQUES RECOMMENDS

1 bottle of Seaport Blush by Woodbury, or if alcohol is prohibited in this public place, 1 bottle of apple cider.

INGREDIENTS

*If Aromantic Seasonings of Seduction is not available in your area, you may use Old Bay® Seasoning.

8 slices of white bread
4 slices of wheat bread
1 loaf of unsliced pumpernickel bread or rye bread
8 oz. soft cream cheese
¼ cup of mayonnaise
4 tablespoons Dijon mustard
1 jar of small capers
½ cup of minced celery
6 medium sweet and sour pickles
1 bunch of seedless black or green grapes
¼ lb. thin sliced honey ham
¼ lb. thin sliced turkey breast
½ teaspoon of Spicy Aromantic Seasonings of Seduction*

PREPARATION

Turkey Roll Sandwiches: Mince until very fine, the turkey and celery and pickles. Mix 4 oz. of cream cheese, 1/8-cup mayonnaise, 2 Tablespoons of Dijon mustard, ¼ teaspoon Aromantic or Old Bay® Seasoning, dash of salt & pepper. Stir above ingredients with a spoon and refrigerate for 15 minutes. Slice bread lengthwise into four, ½-inch thick, slices and remove crust. Spread mixture on slices evenly placing 1 slice at a time on a damp dishtowel. Grab towel on each side of the bread and use towel to slowly roll bread into a 1-inch log. Keep it in the towel for 5 minutes then wrap in wax paper and refrigerate until ready to slice. Slice into one-inch thick slices, wrap in Saran wrap and pack it in picnic basket.

Ham and Capers: Mince ham very fine. Drain capers. Mix remaining ingredients, except for the grapes and stir. Refrigerate for 15 minutes. On 4 slices of white bread, spread mixture evenly. Place one slice of wheat bread on top of white bread and spread mixture on this slice. Top with remaining slice of white bread. (You will end up with 4 sandwiches, each sandwich will be a triple sandwich). Wrap in wax paper and refrigerate until ready to slice. Before cutting into 4 pieces, slice off crust on all four sides. If you prefer, you can cut into triangles, by cutting from corner to corner rather than cutting into 4 squares.

PREPARATION TIME

30 Minutes

PRESENTATION

The usual picnic basket contains a tablecloth, napkins, utensils, wineglasses, a corkscrew and a set of medium lunch plates. We also suggest you take along a large platter so you can arrange your canapés and grapes artistically.

 MASTER CHEF COMMENTS

May you be blessed with a glorious day in the sunny outdoors. It will match the warmth in your hearts. And will your companion think it is sentimental?

But of course!

Love Bites ❦ A Cookbook For Romantic Encounters

_____

_____

_____

_____

_____

_____

_____

_____

_____

_____

_____

_____

Love Bite No. 9
(The Morning After)

SETTING

The setting for this Love Bite is in the bedroom, the morning after a romantic encounter. The morning after can sometimes be intriguing or even questionable. You may think, "Will they love me in the morning?"

CREATE THE MOOD

We suggest you carry the romantic mood from the night before, over to the morning with a special Love Bite romance that is tender, sweet and just a bit different. As you first get up, whisper softly into your companion's ear that you insist he or she remain in bed because you have a surprise but you need a few moments. Follow that with a gentle kiss as you leave the bedroom.

LOVE BITE MENU

- Raspberry Christo
- Champagne Cocktail

Jacques Recommends

1 bottle of Woodbury Chautauqua Champagne is perfect because it's dry and refreshing to the palate. 8 ounces orange juice.

Ingredients

4 slices of thick sandwich bread
   (white or whole wheat)
2 eggs
2 tablespoons of milk
Dash of nutmeg
2 oz. soft cream cheese
2 oz. raspberry preserves
Dash of salt
2 oz. of butter

Preparation

Chill Champagne and orange juice, Beat eggs and milk. Add salt and nutmeg and set aside. Spread cream cheese evenly on 2 slices of bread. On the other 2 slices of bread spread the raspberry preserves. Form a sandwich with 1 slice of each. Using butcher string, tie each sandwich individually across both sides of the sandwich (as you would tie a square box). Heat half the butter in a frying pan over medium heat. Dip the sandwich into the egg mixture and place in the frying pan. Cook one sandwich at a time on both sides until golden brown. Remove from pan, and place on a paper towel to absorb the fat. Repeat for the other sandwich. To serve, remove strings and cut in 4 pieces.

PREPARATION TIME

20 Minutes

PRESENTATION

Display sandwiches on a plate sprinkled with powdered sugar or fresh berries in season. Garnish with a couple of orange slices.

Mix 1/3 orange juice in champagne glass with 2/3 of Champagne.

 MASTER CHEF COMMENTS

The morning after, will this B.I.L.Y. Love Bite, brighten your day?

But of course!

_____

_____

_____

_____

_____

_____

_____

_____

_____

_____

_____

_____

Love Bite No. 10
(Any Time My Love)

SETTING

This Love Bite could take place on a Wednesday night on the living room floor surrounded by pillows in front of the coffee table.

CREATE THE MOOD

The entire room is dark. Place ten or twelve votive candles around the coffee table. Turn on soft romantic music. A string quartet collection might be nice. Remember, there is no special day or night for Love Bite romances but any weekday night would be a perfect time for a romantic encounter to release some built-up tensions.

LOVE BITE MENU

- Crepes à la Reine
  (French pancakes stuffed with chicken)

JACQUES RECOMMENDS

1 bottle of Woodbury Dry Riesling or Seyval finishes off this elegant Love Bite in style.

INGREDIENTS

*If Aromantic Seasonings of Seduction is not available in your area, you may use Old Bay® Seasoning.

For Filling:
1 medium single chicken breast
½ cup canned sliced mushrooms
½ cup grated Swiss cheese
1 tablespoon butter
1 tablespoon flour
1/8 teaspoon Regular Aromantic Seasonings of
    Seduction*
Pinch of salt
1 teaspoon Dijon mustard
For Crepes:
½ cup flour
½ cup milk
1 large egg
Pinch salt
2 tablespoon oil

PREPARATION

Crepes: Heat 10" non-stick frying pan over medium heat. In a mixing bowl beat egg, milk, salt, mustard and flour. Beat until smooth. Add 1 teaspoon of oil. Add one-half of the mixture into pan and turn the pan around in a circular motion to spread batter into a thin coat. Cook until edges are light brown. Flip over and cook until light brown on the other side. Lay crepe on paper towel to remove oil. Repeat for additional crepe.

Filling: Set oven at 375°. Rub chicken breast with oil. Sprinkle with salt & pepper. Place in oven-proof bowl and bake for 20 minutes. In a small saucepan, melt butter over medium heat, add flour and keep stirring until it thickens. Remove pot from burner and add 2/3 of the Swiss cheese. Stir. Add seasonings and mustard, stir and set aside. Drain mushrooms and add to sauce. Dice chicken breast and add to sauce. Lay one crepe flat; spoon in half the fillings from center and spread around to about 2 inches from border. Roll crepe gently. Place crepes in oven-proof platter, repeat, and sprinkle the Swiss cheese evenly on top of crepes. Bake in oven at 375° for 8 minutes and serve.

PREPARATION TIME

35 Minutes

PRESENTATION

Line serving platter with red cabbage leaves. Cut crepes about 1 inch long and arrange them artistically on platter. Decorate with orange slices or any other fresh slices of fruit or vegetables.

 MASTER CHEF COMMENTS

Will this Love Bite mini-feast work for you?

But of course!

Love Bites ⋦ A Cookbook For Romantic Encounters

_____

_____

_____

_____

_____

_____

_____

_____

_____

_____

_____

_____

Love Bite No. 11
(Romance Italian Style)

SETTING

Think Italian for this Love Bite. The place can be anywhere, but think of ways to make it more Italian in atmosphere.

CREATE THE MOOD

There is a mystical force in the combination of salami, which is the magic of this Love Bite. *We are serious about this.* Italians are known for being great lovers and they cherish their salami. So let's create a romantic presentation. Of course, always with candlelight, and romantic music (Pavarotti would be good). The occasion can be made extra special by presenting your companion with flowers–a single rose or a bunch of daisies, it matters not. It is the thought that will win your partner's heart, whether it is for the first time, or a renewal victory from many years ago.

LOVE BITE MENU

- Italian Hearts à la Salami

JACQUES RECOMMENDS

1 bottle Woodbury's Gold Medal Winner Seaport Red is a soft red wine with fruity aromas and a lively finish.

INGREDIENTS

¼ lb. large thin-sliced Salami
8 slices of sandwich bread, lightly toasted
1½ oz. mayonnaise
1½ oz. Dijon mustard
1 small heart shaped cookie cutter
12 large pitted black olives

PREPARATION

Mix mayonnaise and Dijon mustard together. Slice olives lengthwise in half. Toast sandwich bread lightly and with cookie cutter, cut heart shape into toast slices. You should have approximately 32 small heart shape pieces. Do the same with the salami slices. You should be able to cut 6 salami slices at a time. Spread mixture of mayonnaise and Dijon mustard evenly over each toast. Place a salami heart on top so it matches. Top with a black olive half and serve.

PREPARATION TIME

15 Minutes

PRESENTATION

On a large platter lined with romaine lettuce leaves arrange little hearts artistically. You may also add more olives to the center of the platter. You can use either black olives or other stuffed olives.

 MASTER CHEF COMMENTS

Have we given you just one of the Italian Lovers' secrets?

But of course!

_____

_____

_____

_____

_____

_____

_____

_____

_____

_____

_____

_____

Love Bite No. 12
(Latin Romance)

SETTING

The perfect setting for this Love Bite would be a patio or backyard on a moonlit evening.

CREATE THE MOOD

This romantic Love Bite has a Spanish influence. Place lantern candles around the patio railing or in the yard. Place one on the table and turn Latin type music on for a sensual backdrop. This just may very well set the mood for what might become a wild and exotic Love Bite romance.

LOVE BITE MENU

- Chicken Quesadilla Jose

Jacques Recommends

Fifth of the best Tequila gold

Ingredients

3 fresh limes
4 large fresh flour tortillas
8 oz. salsa
Pinch of salt
1 large chicken breast (or 2 small breasts)
1 red bell pepper
4 tablespoon olive oil
4 oz. Jalapeño Jack Cheese
½ teaspoon cumin
4 oz. Sharp Cheddar Cheese
1 tablespoon Cilantro
1 small Jalapeño pepper, minced

NOTE: Tortilla and salsa can be purchased already made.

Preparation

Heat large frying pan over medium heat. Add ½ tablespoon olive oil. Fry tortilla on both sides until crisp. Repeat until all tortillas are done. Remove excess oil with paper towel. Dice raw chicken breast, red bell pepper and Jalapeño peppers. Heat frying pan to high heat and add olive oil. Add chicken, red bell peppers, cumin, cilantro and salt. Fry 5-6 minutes, stirring constantly. Drain oil and set aside. Set oven to 450°. Mix grated Jalapeño and Cheddar cheeses together and spread evenly on each tortilla using only half the cheese. Spread chicken mixture evenly on tortilla then the rest of cheese. Place tortilla on baking sheet. Bake in oven for 8-10 minutes. Remove as soon as cheese begins to bubble. Cut each tortilla into 6 pieces and serve.

PREPARATION TIME

25 Minutes

PRESENTATION

On a large platter covered with shredded lettuce, arrange pieces artistically. In the center, use a small bowl of salsa for dipping.

 MASTER CHEF COMMENTS

Will this HOT Love Bite heat up your
heart, mind and body?

But of course!

_____

_____

_____

_____

_____

_____

_____

_____

_____

_____

_____

 *Love Bite No. 13*
(Sensuality)

SETTING

A perfect setting for this Love Bite is in the bedroom, very late in the evening.

CREATE THE MOOD

Of course, candlelight and romantic music will put you in the mood for this light Love Bite. Roses would be appropriate also. Because the menu is light, the later in the evening the better for this special Love Bite.

LOVE BITE MENU

- Avocado with Caviar

Jacques Recommends

1 bottle of Woodbury's Barrel Fermented
Chardonnay. This spectacular white wine is
fermented and aged in small oak casks. It is soft
and buttery with a hint of citrus. It is one of the
top of the line wines that go well with caviar.

Ingredients

*If Aromantic
Seasonings of
Seduction is
not available
in your area,
you may use
Old Bay®
Seasoning.

2 small ripe avocados

2 oz. of black or red caviar

1 box whole grain crackers

4 drops of Tabasco® sauce

1/8 teaspoon Regular Aromantic Seasonings of
      Seduction *

1/8 teaspoon salt

2 oz. lemon juice

Preparation

Cut avocado in half and remove stone. Scoop out
meat without breaking skins. Place all the
ingredients, except the caviar and crackers in a
blender or food processor. Blend until smooth.
Refill the avocado skins with the avocado mixture
to a mound in the center leaving ½ inch flat
around the edges so you can spoon caviar all
around the filling.

Preparation Time

10 Minutes

You may shred lettuce to fill two salad bowls half full. This will provide a resting bed for the avocado. Carefully place two avocado halves in each bowl and place the salad bowl on an under plate or dinner plate. Arrange crackers all around the bowl and serve.

 MASTER CHEF COMMENTS

This late Love Bite romance is light and sensual. It's colorful and very tasty but will it entice you to share tender and intimate moments together?

But of course!

 # Love Bite No. 14
(Spice of Love)

SETTING

If your companion's spirit is down just a bit, this Love Bite is perfect set in the living room around a coffee table.

CREATE THE MOOD

Lots of pillows around the floor, candlelight (scented candles to lift the spirit – Lavender is good for this) and a single red rose. Make sure the music in the background is uplifting, but romantic. This is not the time for melancholy love songs. New age music will help keep the spirit afloat during this Love Bite.

LOVE BITE MENU

• Shrimp Dijon

JACQUES RECOMMENDS

Woodbury's Seaport White, a special blend of Seyval and Cayuga, will make this Love Bite one to remember.

INGREDIENTS

*If Aromantic Seasonings of Seduction is not available in your area, you may use Old Bay® Seasoning.

10 large fresh shrimp
½ cup fresh cream (35%)
2 tablespoons oil
2 tablespoons Dijon mustard
Pinch salt
2 tablespoons flour
1/8 teaspoon Spicy Aromantic Seasonings of Seduction*
2 medium slices of French bread
Parsley
1 lemon

PREPARATION

Peel and devein shrimp. Leave tails on and rinse in cold water. Dry with paper towel. Dust with flour. In a large frying pan, heat oil on medium heat and add shrimp. Cook them on both sides for 3 minutes on each side. Drain oil from pan. Push shrimp around the pan leaving the center free. Add cream and bring to a boil. Cook two minutes. Add mustard, seasonings and salt. Stir constantly. When sauce is thickened, gently stir in shrimp. Stir for 2 minutes and serve.

PREPARATION TIME

20 Minutes

PRESENTATION

The best way to serve this delicacy is to divide
shrimp and sauce evenly on two dinner plates.
Garnish with lemon wedges and parsley. Arrange
chunks of French bread in a basket or side plate.
Dipping the bread into the sauce of this Love Bite
is delightful.

 MASTER CHEF COMMENTS

This Love Bite is rich in presentation and content.
Is it fair to say the more often you enjoy Love Bite romances,
the more enriched your love life will be?

But of course!

_____

_____

_____

_____

_____

_____

_____

_____

_____

_____

_____

_____

_____

 *Love Bite No. 15*
(Têtê a Têtê)

SETTING

A cool evening under the stars on a patio or backyard would be a good setting for this Love Bite.

CREATE THE MOOD

This Love Bite is designed to bring you and your companion close together. Surround the area with lantern candles and classical music (Vivaldi would be a nice change of pace) and let the event begin!

LOVE BITE MENU

- Filet Mignon Fondue

JACQUES RECOMMENDS

Perhaps you will choose Glacier Ridge Red from Woodbury. It is their dry red wine blend of Ruby Cabernet, Cabernet Franc and Merlot.

INGREDIENTS

8 oz. of center cut Black Angus filet of beef
Marinade:
3 tablespoons olive oil
½ teaspoon Spicy Aromatic Seasonings of
    Seduction*
1 tablespoon Worcestershire sauce
½ teaspoon salt
2 tablespoons red wine
1 - 4 oz. jar horseradish sauce
8 oz. olive oil
8 oz. peanut oil
Parsley
2 Croissant rolls (crescent bread)
3 oz. Dijon mustard
3 oz. mayonnaise
1 oz. honey

*If Aromatic Seasonings of Seduction is not available in your area, you may use Old Bay® Seasoning.

PREPARATION

A fondue pot is a good thing to have on hand for many different recipes. Also, it comes with fondue forks. Cut beef filets in one-inch squares or smaller if you prefer, but not less than ¾ of an inch. Mix marinade (Olive oil, seasonings, Worcestershire sauce, salt, red wine) in a small bowl. Add filet of beef, mix thoroughly and marinate for 30 minutes stirring beef cubes every 10 minutes. Add olive and peanut oil to fondue pot and heat over medium heat for 7 to 8 minutes. Remove before it begins smoking. Place fondue pot on fondue stand and light using Sterno or candle or plug in, depending on your type of fondue pot. Mix Dijon mustard, mayonnaise and honey in a small dipping bowl. Pour horseradish sauce in another dipping bowl.

PREPARATION TIME

35 Minutes

PRESENTATION

Place hot fondue pot on patio table. Surround the pot with dips, and croissants. Drain filet of beef cubes and dry with paper towels. Arrange them on a small platter garnished with parsley springs. Insert a piece of beef on fondue fork and let it cook in oil for 3 to 4 minutes.

 MASTER CHEF COMMENTS

This fondue is superb for getting people close. Will this tête a tête Love Bite romance excite you and your companion?

But of course!

_____

_____

_____

_____

_____

_____

_____

_____

_____

_____

_____

_____

Love Bite No. 16
(International Romance)

SETTING

This fondue Love Bite has an indoor setting. Again, the living room coffee table makes a cozy place to stimulate each other.

CREATE THE MOOD

Light some candles and play international romantic music such as Latin Flamingo or Middle Eastern belly-dancing music or perhaps Oriental love songs. To make this Love Bite more comfortable, try placing fluffy pillows around your table. This international favorite is bound to stimulate your appetite for passion, as well.

LOVE BITE MENU

- International Cheese Fondue

Jacques Recommends

1 bottle of Woodbury's Seyval or Seaport White make this Love Bite more flavorful and well-balanced.

Ingredients

1 demi-baguette of French bread
½ cup Chablis
1 tablespoon Worcestershire sauce
¼ lb. Swiss cheese
¼ lb. Roquefort cheese
¼ lb. Jalapeño Jack cheese

Preparation

Cut French bread into 1-inch cubes. Grate or chop all the cheese into small pieces. Place wine, Worcestershire sauce and cheeses in fondue pot over medium heat. Cook slowly, stirring constantly until cheese is melted. Remove from burner and install fondue pot on fondue stand. Light Sterno or candle under pot.

Preparation Time

20 Minutes

PRESENTATION

On a large serving platter, deposit fondue pot in center. Display bread cubes on both sides. Make yourself comfortable on pillows and begin sipping wine. Insert a piece of bread on fondue fork and let it soak in cheese for 30 seconds. Lift, twist around and enjoy every Love Bite.

 ## MASTER CHEF COMMENTS

Cheese is internationally used as a Love Bite.
Is life good or not?

But of course!

_____

_____

_____

_____

_____

_____

_____

_____

_____

_____

_____

_____

Love Bite No. 17
(Romance À La Suisse)

SETTING

The perfect setting for this Love Bite would be in front of a fireplace in your living room or family room. If you do not have a fireplace however, that reliable coffee table will serve just as well for this fondue Love Bite we are sharing with you.

CREATE THE MOOD

If you have a fireplace, then the flame and smell of the wood burning will enhance the mood for this Love Bite. As usual, soft music in the background is a must. If you do not have a fireplace aromatic fragrances of incense or simmering pot will work just as well.

LOVE BITE MENU

- Swiss Fondue au Chocolat

Jacques Recommends

1 bottle of chilled Cherry or Red Renard from Woodbury is truly a nectar of the gods that blend well with this Love Bite making it delightful.

Ingredients

8 oz. semi-sweet baker dark chocolate
8 oz. semi-sweet Swiss white chocolate
1 large red delicious apple
1 large pear
1 large banana
1 star fruit
8 large ripe strawberries
2 tablespoons light corn syrup
2 oz. brandy

Preparation

Peel apple and pear and remove cores. Cut into ½ inch cubes. Place in a small mixing bowl. Cut lemon and squeeze juice over fruit and let stand for ten minutes. Peel banana and cut into ½ inch slices. Wash star fruit and slice into 1/4-inch thick pieces. Wash and remove stems of strawberries and dry with paper towel. First, break chocolates into small sectional pieces and place in double boiler and cook until chocolate is melted. You may use the fondue pot as the top part of the double boiler. Stir and add corn syrup and brandy. Continue to stir. Light up Sterno or candle under the fondue pot and it's ready.

PREPARATION TIME

20 Minutes

PRESENTATION

Set fondue pot in center of a large tray or serving platter. Drain and dry apple and pear cubes. Display all fruits around the tray or platter. Make yourself comfortable and begin sipping wine or champagne bubbly. Insert one piece of fruit on fondue fork. Dip in chocolate for 10 seconds. Lift, twist, and give it a few seconds to cool, then let your hair down.

 MASTER CHEF COMMENTS

Ancient Inca Indians believed that chocolate was an aphrodisiac. Is this a romantic Love Bite or not?

But of course!

_____

_____

_____

_____

_____

_____

_____

_____

_____

_____

_____

_____

Love Bite No. 18
(Under the Stars)

SETTING

The patio or garden setting, under bright stars on a summer night makes the perfect place for this Love Bite romance.

CREATE THE MOOD

Lantern candles, and a CD or cassette with nature sounds (the sound of waves and waterfalls would be perfect for this one) will only enhance this Love Bite.

LOVE BITE MENU

- Ocean Hot Pot

JACQUES RECOMMENDS

1 bottle of Woodbury's Brut Champagne makes this Love Bite just a bit more special.

INGREDIENTS

1 bottle of clam juice
1 can of chicken broth
½ tablespoon salt
1 teaspoon Old Bay® Seasoning
1 bay leaf
½ cup dry sherry
1 can of fresh oysters (approximately 15 oz.)
1 bottle of cocktail sauce
1 lemon
12 saltine crackers

PREPARATION

Add clam juice, chicken broth, sherry, seasonings, salt and bay leaf in fondue pot and bring to a boil. Remove from burner and light burner under fondue stand. Place fondue pot on top. Rinse oysters under cold water, drain and place on a serving platter. Pour cocktail sauce in dipping bowl.

PREPARATION TIME

15 Minutes

PRESENTATION

Place fondue pot in center of tray or large serving
platter. On one side, display oysters on lettuce
leaves with lemon wedges. On the other side put
cocktail sauce and display crackers. Insert one
oyster on fondue fork and cook for one or two
minutes and enjoy.

NOTE: Save this broth in a plastic container for
a few days or freeze it for a future Love Bite
occasion. Can be used with clams, fish morsels,
scallops, shrimp or any other fish.

 MASTER CHEF COMMENTS

Love Bites have certainly put a lot of fun and
activity into their romances using the Fondue pot.
Do you see how much you can enjoy each other
as you share the fondue experience?

But of course!

_____

_____

_____

_____

_____

_____

_____

_____

_____

_____

_____

_____

Love Bite No. 19
(The Fire of Love)

SETTING

This Love Bite setting can be both functional and romantic if you have a wood-burning fireplace. Don't despair if there is no fireplace because you can use your oven broiler to prepare the Love Bite. Then, the good news is you can choose any place you want to enjoy it. Perhaps you will even choose the bedroom!

CREATE THE MOOD

If you have a fireplace, the fire crackling and the soft romantic music in the background, creates a relaxing mood. Using pillows or beanbags to sit on or to lie side-by-side will make this Love Bite very special. Something different is not only fun, but it can be entertaining and romantic.

LOVE BITE MENU

- Pioneers' Shish-Kabob

Jacques Recommends

1 bottle of Woodbury's Merlot aged in oak casks fits this Love Bite perfectly. It is smooth and silky with hints of black cherry and a long fruit finish.

Ingredients

*If Aromantic Seasonings of Seduction is not available in your area, you may use Old Bay® Seasonings

1 – 14 oz. 1-inch thick New York cut strip
    Black Angus steak
12 fresh mushrooms
1 yellow small bell pepper
1 green small bell pepper
4 oz. horseradish sauce
French bread (optional)
Marinade:
3 oz. olive oil
1 oz. lemon juice
1 tablespoon Worcestershire sauce
1 teaspoon Spicy Aromantic Seasonings of
    Seduction*
4 dashes Tabasco® sauce
Pinch of rosemary

Preparation

Trim all the fat from beef and cut into 1-inch squares. Place marinade in mixing bowl and add beef cubes. Mix thoroughly. Wash and cut yellow and green bell peppers into 1-inch squares and add to marinade. Wipe mushrooms clean and remove stems. Add to marinade for 20 minutes. Mix a couple times while it is marinating.

Preparation Time

20 Minutes

Love Bites ❧ A Cookbook For Romantic Encounters

PRESENTATION

For the next step, you can use your fireplace but only if it is wood burning. Most fireplace utensils have a long fork. If not, use your two-prong barbecue fork. Make sure the utensil is clean. On a platter, place the mixing bowl of beef and vegetables. Pour horseradish sauce into a dipping bowl. Place French bread around the bowl if you choose to use bread. Insert one piece of green pepper, followed by one beef cube, one yellow pepper, one beef cub, one mushroom and finally a green pepper on the end. Do this on both prongs of the long fork. Move one side of the fire screen a little and choose a spot over brazier where there is not much flame. Keep turning fork slowly as you are sipping wine and romancing. It takes 3 to 5 minutes for the shishkabob to cook.

NOTE: If you don't have a wood-burning fireplace, cook kabobs under the oven broiler approximately 4 to 5 minutes. Make sure to turn them around two or three times. *Voila!* This Love Bite is very romantic and quite rewarding.

 MASTER CHEF COMMENTS

With this Love Bite, you may find you and your companion still in front of the fireplace in the early morning hours. Don't you agree that it will not matter that the fire went out in the fireplace because you will still feel the warmth of this exciting romantic Love Bite?

But of course!

_____

_____

_____

_____

_____

_____

_____

_____

_____

_____

_____

Love Bite No. 20
(Love Break)

SETTING

Timing is everything for the setting on this Love Bite. This is a love break time. You know…in between love making sessions. It will renew your supply of energy. So, the setting is of course, the bedroom.

CREATE THE MOOD

Scented candles fill the room with fragrances of fresh flowers, or perhaps citrus aromas. Play soft music in the background that reminds you and your companion of some far off place, away from the familiarity of your everyday routines.

LOVE BITE MENU

- Bleu-Crab Stuffed Mushroom Caps

JACQUES RECOMMENDS

1 Bottle chilled Barrel Fermented Chardonnay, well-balanced with lemon, pear and vanilla aromas, titillate the senses in this Love Bite.

INGREDIENTS

*If Aromantic Seasonings of Seduction is not available in your area, you may use Old Bay® Seasoning.

¼ lb. bleu-crab meat

4 oz. grated Swiss cheese

2 tablespoons bread crumbs

2 tablespoons chopped fresh cilantro or parsley

1/8 teaspoon cayenne pepper

¼ teaspoon Spicy Aromantic Seasonings of Seduction*

Pinch of salt

6 large mushroom caps

4 tablespoons olive oil

6 Melba toast slices

½ lb. grapes

PREPARATION

Set oven at 400°. Wipe mushroom caps clean and remove stems. Mix together grated cheese, breadcrumbs, cilantro, seasonings, cayenne pepper, and salt. Remove all cartilage and pieces of shell from crabmeat but leave lumps whole. Add to mixture and mix gently. Fill mushroom caps using all crab mixture. Place mushroom caps in oven-proof baking casserole. Pour olive oil on top and bake for 12 to 15 minutes until golden brown.

PREPARATION TIME

25 Minutes

PRESENTATION

Cover dinner plate with romaine lettuce leaves.
Put three mushroom caps on each plate. Arrange
Melba toast around the mushrooms. Garnish
with grapes. Make a romantic toast to your
companion and enjoy this Love Bite romance.

 MASTER CHEF COMMENTS

With this recipe, should you be energized?

But of course!

_____

_____

_____

_____

_____

_____

_____

_____

_____

_____

_____

_____

 # Love Bite No. 21
(Love À La Française)

SETTING

This Love Bite is very French and the best setting or this would be in the bedroom. If you have a parlor or sitting area in the bedroom, start the Love Bite there and before you know it, well...

CREATE THE MOOD

French love songs in the background or other sensuous music should be suitable for this romance. Light a single white taper candle and lay two red roses across one another beside the wineglasses.

LOVE BITE MENU

- Oysters Goulash in Puff Pastry

JACQUES RECOMMENDS

1 bottle of Woodbury's Barrel Fermented Chardonnay will enhance this Love Bite.

INGREDIENTS

*If Aromantic Seasonings of Seduction is not available in your area, you may use Old Bay® Seasoning.

1 box of frozen puff pastry shells
(these can be found at any supermarket)
8 oz. fresh oysters
¼ cup red bell pepper, chopped fine
¼ cup celery, chopped fine
2 tablespoons chopped parsley
2 tablespoons butter
1 tablespoon flour
½ teaspoon of Spicy Aromantic Seasonings of
Seduction*
Pinch of salt
Pinch of nutmeg
¼ cup fresh cream

PREPARATION

Set oven at 400°. Remove two frozen pastry shells. Read box instructions. Reseal remaining shells and store in freezer. Pastry shells can be baked in advance but it should not take more than 30 minutes to bake. In a large skillet, melt butter. Add peppers and celery and sauté 4 minutes. Add flour and cook 2 or 3 minutes more. Add oysters with its liquid. Add seasonings, nutmeg, and salt. Cook over medium heat for 5 minutes. Add cream slowly, continuing to stir. Add 2/3 of the parsley. When sauce is thickened, remove from burner. Place one pastry shell on each dinner plate. Remove cap of pastry shells by inserting a small pointed knife in the circle and lift up. Remove soft pastry inside and discard. Fill pastry shells with mixture evenly. It will overflow but that is okay. Replace pastry shell caps and sprinkle with parsley and serve.

PREPARATION TIME

35 Minutes

PRESENTATION

The filled pastry shells arranged on a dinner plate is all it takes to make this delicious Love Bite awaken the heart to romance.

 MASTER CHEF COMMENTS

Along with a good bottle of Woodbury wine, what will follow this Love Bite is your personal romantic efforts and…and…and…

But of course!

_____

_____

_____

_____

_____

_____

_____

_____

_____

_____

_____

_____

Love Bite No. 22
(Mediterranean Romance)

SETTING

This is quick and easy, so this Love Bite would be perfect for the bedroom.

CREATE THE MOOD

Create a Mediterranean ambiance with music featuring stringed instruments or melodic love songs. Create the feeling of the "Love Boat" by using festive and romantic decorations. Petals from roses strewn all over the bed and/or placing a row of votive candles in front of the dresser mirror creates a nice effect as the double images flicker and charge the room with magic.

LOVE BITE MENU

- Mango Wrapped in Prosciutto

Jacques Recommends

Woodbury Seaport Blush, which is similar to White Zinfandel with a delicate hue and fragrant bouquet. Riesling is another exceptional vintage on the sweet side with intense fruit and floral aromas. Either way you can't go wrong!

Ingredients

*If Aromantic Seasonings of Seduction is not available in your area, you may use Old Bay® Seasoning.

¼ lb. thinly sliced Prosciutto Italian ham
1 large ripe mango
1 small jar of capers
4 oz. soft cream cheese
6 sesame breadsticks
Pinch of nutmeg
Pinch of Spicy Aromantic Seasonings of
    Seduction*
½ lb. grapes
1 small package fresh mint leaves

Preparation

Trim fat from Prosciutto. Peel mango and cut lengthwise in half-inch strips. This will make about 8 strips. Remove remaining soft mango around the stone and mash it. Mix it with cream cheese and 2 tablespoons drained capers. Spread evenly on Prosciutto slices. Place one mango strip on edge of Prosciutto and roll. You may refrigerate for 10 minutes if you wish.

PREPARATION TIME

15 Minutes

PRESENTATION

Cut Prosciutto rolls in three pieces and place on a platter. Garnish with mint leaves. Arrange several clusters of grapes on the plate. Serve with breadsticks.

 MASTER CHEF COMMENTS

Like we said in the beginning, this is so fast and easy do you suppose it was created by men from around the Mediterranean so they would have more time for the main course of their Love feast?

But of course!

_____

_____

_____

_____

_____

_____

_____

_____

_____

_____

_____

_____

Love Bite No. 23
(Ocean Romance)

SETTING

This is another great outdoor Love Bite romance. Choose the patio, yard, or garden setting in the moonlight.

CREATE THE MOOD

Your portable cassette or CD player will come in handy to help set the mood for this Love Bite. You want to give your companion the feeling of being near the water so definitely play ocean sounds with its forceful waves beating the shore. Lantern candles will provide just enough light to complete the scene.

LOVE BITE MENU

- Clam Bake

JACQUES RECOMMENDS

1 bottle of chilled Woodbury Chardonnay is perfect for this Clambake.

INGREDIENTS

24 small cherrystone clams

4 – 1 inch thick slices of French bread

4 slices Swiss cheese

Paprika

2 bay leaves

1 teaspoon Spicy Aromantic Seasonings of Seduction*

1 cup of dry Sherry

1 lemon

½ lb. butter

Parsley

1 teaspoon salt

*If Aromantic Seasonings of Seduction is not available in your area, you may use Old Bay® Seasoning.

PREPARATION

In a large pot add 1 cup water, 1 cup dry sherry, salt, bay leaves and seasonings. Bring to a boil over high heat. Scrub clam shells and rinse 2 or 3 times in cold water. Add to boiling pot, cover and steam for 5 to 6 minutes. Remove from burner as soon as clams begin to open. Set oven at 450°. Put one slice of Swiss cheese on top of French bread slices. Place on baking sheet and cook until cheese is melted. In a small saucepan, melt butter slowly. Pour gently only the butterfat into a small dipping bowl. For garnish, add parsley and cut lemons in wedges.

PREPARATION TIME

15 Minutes

PRESENTATION

Place clams in the center of a large platter.
Arrange lemon wedges around the platter. Place
two French bread slices on each individual plate
and set the butter-dipping bowl between you.

 MASTER CHEF COMMENTS

Should this Love Bite Romance
become a frequent one?

But of course!

_____

_____

_____

_____

_____

_____

_____

_____

_____

_____

_____

_____

Love Bite No. 24
(Elegance)

SETTING

The living room in front of the fireplace
(optional) makes a great setting for this Love Bite.

CREATE THE MOOD

Soft music (perhaps Bocelli) in the background
will set the stage for this sophisticated and
romantic Love Bite. A candelabra on the hearth
(or on the coffee table) will set the stage for the
elegant Love Bite menu.

NOTE: If you don't have a candelabra then tall
tapers will also do the trick. The affect you are
trying to achieve is elegance.

LOVE BITE MENU

- Alaskan King Crab Legs Fantasy

JACQUES RECOMMENDS

1 bottle of Chardonnay or Dry Riesling, chilled
give this Love Bite unforgettable style.

INGREDIENTS

*If Aromantic Seasonings of Seduction is not available in your area, you may use Old Bay® Seasoning.

1½ lb. Alaskan King Crab Legs

1 demi-baguette French bread

¼ cup mayonnaise

¼ cup Dijon mustard

1 oz. Brandy

¼ cup minced fresh parsley

½ teaspoon Spicy Aromantic Seasonings of Seduction*

2 oz. lemon juice

PREPARATION

In a large pot, add two quarts of water and lemon juice. Bring to a boil. Cut crab legs in middle joints and add to boiling pot. Cook 5 minutes and remove from pot. With a big knife cut crab legs lengthwise and remove all crabmeat from shells. Remove center bones. Place on a serving platter and keep warm. Set oven at 400°. Place bread in oven for 7 minutes. Mix mayonnaise, Dijon mustard, Brandy and seasonings in a bowl and beat until smooth. Pour into dipping bowl and serve.

PREPARATION TIME

15 Minutes

PRESENTATION

Place crab leg meat on a medium-size decorative platter. Place dipping bowl in the center of the platter. Cut bread into 2-inch pieces and place on individual plates.

 MASTER CHEF COMMENTS

This Love Bite is definitely a keeper!
Will you use it many times?

But of course!

_____

_____

_____

_____

_____

_____

_____

_____

_____

_____

_____

_____

 *Love Bite No. 25*
(Aphrodisiac)

SETTING

The living room couch works well for this Love Bite but we just know you will slip down to the floor, surround yourselves with lots of pillows and use the coffee table.

CREATE THE MOOD

This Love Bite definitely calls for Yanni-type music. And with Yanni-type music in the background, you don't need much more. For good measure though, scented candles or incense can heighten the mood.

LOVE BITE MENU

- Lobster au Pernod®

JACQUES RECOMMENDS

1 Fifth of French Pernod®

INGREDIENTS

1 – 12 oz. Rock Lobster tail
1 – 8 oz. can of Hearts of Palm
8 oz. fresh cream (35%)
2 tablespoons butter
2 oz. Pernod®
1 tablespoon Dijon mustard
½ teaspoon Spicy Aromatic Seasonings of
    Seduction*
Pinch of nutmeg
Pinch of salt
4 drops of Tabasco® sauce
2 tablespoons flour
2 – 2 inch thick French bread slices,
    warmed in oven

*If Aromatic Seasonings of Seduction is not available in your area, you may use Old Bay® Seasoning.

PREPARATION

Before you prepare this meal, fix two Pernod®
cocktails. In a cocktail glass filled with ice cubes
add 1 ½ oz. Pernod® and fill glass with water.
Enjoy! Use a big knife and laying lobster tail on
its back on a cutting board, cut lobster tail
lengthwise in the middle. Separate meat from
shell (reserve shell). Cut lobster meat in 1-inch
slices. First remove black vein and put lobsters on
plate. Dust pieces with flour and set aside. In a
large skillet melt butter over medium heat. Add
lobster and cook for 5 minutes on all sides.

Drain butter and add Pernod®. Stand back and ignite, tossing lobster around the pan. Add cream, hearts of palm, Dijon mustard, seasonings, nutmeg, salt, Tabasco® and stir constantly until thickened. Remove from burner and keep warm.

PREPARATION TIME

20 Minutes

PRESENTATION

In a small pot, bring to boil 2 cups of water and add lobster shells. Remove as soon as shells change color. Drain, split down middle and place in center of two dinner plates. Fill each half of lobster tail evenly. Drizzle sauce over lobster. Serve with warm bread and enjoy, but first prepare another Pernod® cocktail and propose a toast to your companion. "Let the romancing begin!"

 MASTER CHEF COMMENTS

First, you must realize that Pernod® is definitely an aphrodisiac. It is in the family of Absente and can create very arousing effects. Could it be that a Pernod® cocktail is a century old Viagra®?

But of course!

_____

_____

_____

_____

_____

_____

_____

_____

_____

_____

_____

_____

_____

Love Bite No. 26
(Asian Melody)

SETTING

A perfect Love Bite in the bedroom as you lounge around after a romantic encounter.

CREATE A MOOD

Uplifting music (on the romantic side though and preferably Asian) and scented candles will prepare you for this quick and easy Love Bite. If you can find them, placing oriental lanterns throughout the room can add to this festive oriental experience.

LOVE BITE MENU

- Chicks-on-a-Skewer

JACQUES RECOMMENDS

1 bottle of Imperial Sake, warmed.

INGREDIENTS

*If Aromantic Seasonings of Seduction is not available in your area, you may use Old Bay® Seasoning.

8 oz. chicken breast

4 oz. coconut cream (this can be purchased in oriental stores or gourmet shops)

1 teaspoon of yellow curry paste

½ teaspoon Spicy Aromantic Seasonings of Seduction*

Pinch of salt

2 full tablespoons peanut butter

2 oz. sesame oil

Bamboo skewers

1 small bag crispy Chinese noodles

PREPARATION

Cut chicken breast into 2 medium-size pieces and cut into long thick strips. Run bamboo skewers all the way through the chicken strips, weaving it like a ribbon. Lay skewered chicken sticks in a large flat oven-proof casserole. In a small saucepan, heat curry paste over medium heat. Add sesame oil, stir and add coconut cream, peanut butter, seasonings and salt and stir. Cook for two minutes and pour over the row of chicken on the bamboo skewers. Let cool for 15 minutes then press them flat gently with your hand, turn them over and press them gently again. A gas grill is best for cooking this Love Bite but if you do not have one, set broiler pan in oven and move grill as close to broiler as possible. Broil skewers on both sides for one minute. Serve with a small bowl of steamed rice but this is optional.

Warming The Sake: In a large pot add 2 quarts of water and bring to boil. Open Sake bottle and immerge bottle ¾ of the way into pot. Turn down burner to lowest heat and leave bottle in hot water until ready to serve. If you have a wine bucket it would be a good idea to fill bucket half full of hot water to keep Sake warm.

PREPARATION TIME

25 Minutes

PRESENTATION

Place skewers on a medium platter lined with crispy Chinese noodles and serve.

 MASTER CHEF COMMENTS

You should pour much sake throughout this Love Bite. Should you trust me when I tell you it will make you feel very exotic?

But of course!

_____

_____

_____

_____

_____

_____

_____

_____

_____

_____

_____

_____

Love Bite No. 27
(Exotic Moonlight)

SETTING

Under the stars on the patio is the setting for this next Love Bite with an oriental flair.

CREATE THE MOOD

Move those oriental lanterns you used in Love Bite No. 26 out to the patio. Strike up the music (oriental of course) and light a few scented candles or incense and get ready for another sensual Love Bite.

LOVE BITE MENU

- Beef Tendori on Skewers

1 Bottle of Sake Imperial (the best).

INGREDIENTS

8 oz. of Black Angus strip steak
(Ask your butcher to slice it into strips about
1/8 of an inch thick) Cut off all the fat.
4 oz. soy sauce
4 tablespoons sugar
1 tablespoon ginger powder
2 tablespoons rice wine vinegar
1 tablespoon cornstarch
2 tablespoons of water
Bamboo skewers

PREPARATION

Insert Bamboo skewers into the center of each
beef strip. Weave the meat onto the stick in
ribbon like fashion. Place the beef skewers in an
oven-proof casserole dish. In a small saucepan
bring to a boil soy sauce, sugar, rice vinegar, and
ginger. Remove from burner and cool. Pour
mixture over beef bamboo skewers and marinate
for 15 minutes. Drain marinade into the small
saucepan and bring to boil. Mix water and
cornstarch and add to marinade. Stir and as it
begins to thicken remove from burner. With a
pastry brush, brush both sides of the beef skewers.
Again, a gas grill broiler will be best suited for
charring because it cools quickly. If a gas grill is
not available set oven broiler at maximum and

broil meat on both sides. Broil about 1 minute, remove and turn over. Brush with mixture again and broil for 1 additional minute.

PREPARATION TIME

30 Minutes

PRESENTATION

In a serving platter lined with lettuce leaves, arrange Tendori . A bowl of steamed rice is optional but do not forget to serve the warm Sake. (Instructions for warming Sake were given in Love Bite 26).

 MASTER CHEF COMMENTS

This Love Bite will definitely please you and your companion. Should you be feeling exotic before the occasion is over?

But of course!

_____

_____

_____

_____

_____

_____

_____

_____

_____

_____

_____

_____

_____

 *Love Bite No. 28*
(Sensual Mood)

SETTING

This Love Bite is intense and requires immediate reaction, so the bedroom is probably the best setting for this sensual menu.

CREATE THE MOOD

Soft music is a must for this event and the softer the better. Just a hint of lavender from a scented candle will create the proper mood for both of you. Perhaps you should use those satin sheets you have been saving for a special occasion. A single rose across your partner's pillow will await him or her upon entering your love nest for this sensual and exciting Love Bite.

LOVE BITE MENU

- Oysters Wrapped in Sunshine

Jacques Recommends

1 bottle of Woodbury Chardonnay, chilled.

Ingredients

*If Aromantic Seasonings of Seduction is not available in your area, you may use Old Bay® Seasoning.

16 oz. fresh oysters
1 large grapefruit
1 teaspoon Spicy Aromantic Seasonings of
    Seduction
4 drops of Tabasco® sauce
½ teaspoon dill weed
½ teaspoon anise seed
1 package of ground wheat crackers

Preparation

Cut grapefruit in half and remove all meat without breaking outside skin. Put contents in blender and add all the other ingredients except the oysters and crackers. Blend until smooth. Pour in a mixing bowl and add oysters and juice. Mix and fill half grapefruit shells and serve.

Preparation Time

15 Minutes

PRESENTATION

Place grapefruit shells into small glass salad bowls.
Serve with crackers.

 MASTER CHEF COMMENTS

This is a HOT HOT HOT Love Bite
romance. If this one does not do the trick for
you then Viagra® is needed. It was my
experience that it was not needed,
so are you too, a player?

But of course!

_____

_____

_____

_____

_____

_____

_____

_____

_____

_____

_____

_____

Love Bite No. 29
(Midweek Romance)

SETTING

The time for this Love Bite romance is much more important than the actual setting. Midweek is the best time for this occasion because sometimes it is then that we run out of energy and don't feel up to…well, you know…we are, exhausted from our life-style demands. This little Love Bite might just do the trick and bring zest back into your life. Kiss those mid-week routines good-bye and your companion hello!

CREATE THE MOOD

Dress the part by wearing something comfortable. A sensuous robe for the woman; a smoking jacket or comfortable bathrobe for the man, will work. Fill the room with the glow of scented candles, add soft music, then lie back and breathe in the aromas. If you feel a bit daring, you might even want to try this Love Bite beside a nice warm tub of foaming essential bath oils. There are lots of things you can do with this Love Bite, so let your imagination lead you down the road to romance. Remember in life–it isn't the destination that matters, but the *journey*.

LOVE BITE MENU

- Continental Cheese Dip

JACQUES RECOMMENDS

1 bottle of Woodbury White Renard, if you like a fruity white wine blend with a sweet, grapey taste, or Riesling, on the sweet side with intense fruit aromas.

INGREDIENTS

*If Aromantic Seasonings of Seduction is not available in your area, you may use Old Bay® Seasoning.

4 oz. Swiss cheese

4 oz. soft cream cheese

1 cup of fresh raspberries

2 tablespoons Sauterne wine

Assorted fresh fruits and if you prefer vegetables
    (but fruits are the more sensual items here)

1 teaspoon Regular Aromantic Seasonings of Seduction*

PREPARATION

Make this one quick and easy. Use the microwave and set on high for 2 minutes. Place cream cheese in a one-quart bowl suitable for the microwave. Grate the Swiss cheese and add it to the bowl stirring the mixture together. Microwave for 2 minutes. Wash and drain raspberries and put in blender. Add wine and seasonings and liquefy at high speed. Pass through a sieve and add to bowl with cheese. Stir and cook for 1 more minute or until mixture is hot and smooth. Pour into a dipping bowl for serving. Wash and cut assorted fruits and vegetables to bite size pieces.

PREPARATION TIME

15 Minutes

PRESENTATION

On a medium-size serving platter, place dipping
bowl in center and arrange the fruits and veggies
around the bowl. *Voila !*

 MASTER CHEF COMMENTS

This is so quick and easy it may even
inspire you for a quickie. Right?

But of course!

_____

_____

_____

_____

_____

_____

_____

_____

_____

_____

_____

 *Love Bite No. 30*
(Love Bite Italiano)

SETTING

This Love Bite will work beautifully on a warm breezy evening on your patio.

CREATE THE MOOD

Let the violins serenade you and your companion as they do in most romantic Italian café settings you see in the movies. Lanterns with flickering candles and wineglasses overflowing with the nectar of the gods will make this a Love Bite to remember.

LOVE BITE MENU

- Stuffed Zucchini Romano

JACQUES RECOMMENDS

1 bottle of Woodbury's Seaport Red, a soft, red wine with fruity aromas and a lively finish make this Love Bite hearty.

INGREDIENTS

*If Aromantic Seasonings of Seduction is not available in your area, you may use Old Bay® Seasoning.

8 oz. of hot Italian sausage

1 large zucchini

2 oz. grated Romano cheese

1 oz. wine

2 oz. grated mozzarella cheese

1 tablespoon olive oil

1 egg

3 tablespoons bread crumbs

½ teaspoon Spicy Aromantic Seasonings of
     Seduction*

2 thick slices of Italian bread

6 cherry tomatoes

1 small package carrot sticks

PREPARATION

Wash and dry the zucchini and cut in center lengthwise. Spoon out center of each half of the zucchini to form a boat. Rub outside generously with olive oil. Place in oven-proof platter and set aside. Set oven at 375º. Remove sausage from casing and add sausage to medium frying pan. Set burner for medium heat and add seasonings. Cook until crumbly, stirring meat constantly. Add 1 oz. wine and reduce heat to low. Cook for 5 minutes. Remove from burner, stir and add

2 tablespoons breadcrumbs, mozzarella cheese, and egg. Stir thoroughly. Fill both centers of zucchini with mixture. Mix 1 tablespoon breadcrumbs and Romano cheese and spread over Zucchini to cover completely. Bake in oven for 18-20 minutes.

PREPARATION TIME

30 Minutes

PRESENTATION

Place zucchini in the center of a dinner plate and garnish with cherry tomatoes and julienne carrots. Serve with one slice of Italian bread.

 MASTER CHEF COMMENTS

Love Bite Italiano should do the trick and
I am sure you will add a few romantic tricks
of your own, will you not?

But of course!

_____

_____

_____

_____

_____

_____

_____

_____

_____

_____

_____

_____

Love Bite No. 31
(Drums of Africa)

SETTING

This Love Bite romance is from the southeastern part of Africa. It will certainly awaken your sexual appetite because your bloodstream may reach a boiling point. Impatience to move on to a hot night of passion, makes the bedroom definitely the right place for this Love Bite.

CREATE THE MOOD

The sounds of drums beating can be erotic so this might be the best music to have in the background. Nature sounds will work as well. Ravel's *Bolero* would definitely be a good choice here also. Scented candles or musk incense, which arouse the senses would not be wasted here.

LOVE BITE MENU

- Chicken Afrique

JACQUES RECOMMENDS

1 bottle of Woodbury Seaport Blush will bring out the color in your partner's cheeks.

INGREDIENTS

*If Aromantic Seasonings of Seduction is not available in your area, you may use Old Bay® Seasoning.

2 medium single chicken breast

2 tablespoons flour

1 teaspoon Spicy Aromantic Seasonings of Seduction*

1 teaspoon crushed black pepper

½ teaspoon savory

½ teaspoon salt

2 oz. Olive oil

4 tablespoons marmalade

4 tablespoons Dijon mustard

2 tablespoons mayonnaise

PREPARATION

Mix flour well with every spice and seasoning in recipe. Pour this onto a flat platter. Lay both Chicken breasts on top and cover both sides thoroughly with mixture. Let stand for 10 minutes. Set oven at 400°. Add olive oil to a large skillet and heat to medium temperature. Fry chicken breast on both sides to a light brown. Remove from frying pan and place chicken breast onto an oven-proof platter. Bake for 15 minutes. Mix Dijon mustard, marmalade and mayonnaise. Cook in a small saucepan until hot but not boiling (about 2 minutes). Stir constantly. Put dipping sauce in a bowl. Cut chicken breast in ½ inch squares.

PREPARATION TIME

25 Minutes

PRESENTATION

Line a medium-size serving platter with endive leaves. Put dipping bowl in center and arrange chicken pieces around it.

 MASTER CHEF COMMENTS

This Love Bite romance promises to be one of the HOTTEST ones you will ever try. It's great if your relationship needs a boost. Should you do this again?

But of course!

_____

_____

_____

_____

_____

_____

_____

_____

_____

_____

_____

_____

Love Bite No. 32
(You Are Special)

SETTING

The setting for this Love Bite romance will be well suited for the living room.

CREATE THE MOOD

Candlelight and soft, romantic background music will set the stage for your presentation of a single red rose to your companion. Any flower will do, even a single daisy. The message here is "I think you are special".

Breaking routines really helps in keeping balance in your sexual life. This is the intent of Love Bites romance ideas.

LOVE BITE MENU

- Shrimp-on-a-Skewer

JACQUES RECOMMENDS

1 chilled bottle of Woodbury's Chardonnay aged in American oak, is well balanced with lemon, pear and vanilla aromas.

INGREDIENTS

10 jumbo raw shrimp

1 lime

1 teaspoon Spicy Aromantic Seasonings of Seduction*

2 oz. olive oil

¼ teaspoon salt

Pinch of cayenne pepper

1 small can of pineapple rings

1 oz. dry sherry

2 thick slices of French bread

Bamboo skewers

*If Aromantic Seasonings of Seduction is not available in your area, you may use Old Bay® Seasoning.

PREPARATION

Peel and devein shrimp. Leave tails on. Rinse in cold water and pat dry. In a medium bowl, mix together olive oil, fresh squeezed lime juice, sherry, seasonings, cayenne and salt. Add shrimp and mix thoroughly several times during the marinating process. Set gas grill or oven broiler on high. Cut each pineapple ring in four wedges. Arrange one piece of pineapple on bamboo skewer followed by one shrimp. Repeat until bamboo skewer holds 3 shrimp and 4 pieces of pineapple.

NOTE: If you use longer bamboo skewers, you may be able to put 5 shrimp on each one.

Broil shrimp until pink in color. Brush with marinade on all sides and return to broiler. Approximately 8 to 10 minutes cooking time.

NOTE: If oven broiler is used it is a good idea to place skewers on a rack on top of oven-proof platter. Baste often. You may also warm bread if you wish.

PREPARATION TIME

20 Minutes

PRESENTATION

Line a medium-size platter with shredded lettuce. Place shrimp-on-a-skewer across platter with bread on both ends and serve.

 MASTER CHEF COMMENTS

I found a lot of excitement with this Love Bite romance. It seemed to put me in the mood. Should it do the same for you?

But of course!

_____

_____

_____

_____

_____

_____

_____

_____

_____

_____

_____

Love Bite No. 33
(Winter in New Orleans)

SETTING

If the weather is cold and rainy outside, then the perfect setting for this Love Bite is at the living room coffee table. If you have a fireplace, light the fire and prepare for a magical Love Bite.

CREATE THE MOOD

Put New Orleans Jazz music on and prepare for a Cajun Love Bite. It can be dreary outside, but the mood you create inside with the music and the bubbly lets you throw your cares to the wind.

LOVE BITE MENU

- Crawfish Tails on Toast

Jacques Recommends

1 bottle of Chardonnay or Dry Riesling, chilled will help cool you down with this Love Bite.

Ingredients

*If Aromantic Seasonings of Seduction is not available in your area, you may use Old Bay® Seasoning.

8 oz. Crawfish tails
½ cup diced red bell peppers
¼ teaspoon Spicy Aromantic Seasonings of Seduction*
1 tablespoon fresh chopped basil
1/8 teaspoon ground clove
1/8 teaspoon ground black pepper
1/8 teaspoon cayenne pepper
1½ tablespoons butter
¼ teaspoon salt
1 tablespoon flour
1 cup fresh cream (35%)
1 lemon
2 slices of whole wheat toast

Preparation

In a medium frying pan, melt butter over medium heat. Add bell peppers. Cook 2 minutes. Peel and devein Crawfish and add to the pan. Cut lemon in half. Squeeze juice of one half of lemon in pan. Add all seasonings and spices. Stir and cook 2 minutes. Stir in flour and cook 1 minute. Add cream, stirring constantly. When sauce thickens remove from burner. Trim edges of toasts and cut into triangles.

PREPARATION TIME

    25 Minutes

PRESENTATION

On two small dinner plates arrange toast so the triangle points face rim of plate, forming a square in the center of the plate. Divide crawfish in two. Place in center of squares with slices of lemon for garnish.

 MASTER CHEF COMMENTS

If it happens that your romantic partner is on the cold side, well believe me it will not be for long. After a few mouthfuls of this Love Bite, you may be getting Love Bites. Should you believe me?

But of course!

_____

_____

_____

_____

_____

_____

_____

_____

_____

_____

_____

_____

_____

Love Bite No. 34
(For An Encore)

SETTING

We have given you a lot of ideas for settings for romantic encounters in this cookbook. Perhaps you can move from room to room with the finale in the bedroom for this Love Bite.

CREATE THE MOOD

Lingerie, lingerie, and more lingerie…that will set the mood along with the wispy, wily, sensual music in the background for this Love Bite. (Try one of the three B's – Bacharach, Beethoven or Bellafonte). We suggest layers of lingerie, so that as the Love Bite progresses you can unveil, piece by piece, thus adding heightened anticipation to the pleasure of the moment ahead. For the male partner, a simple robe is all that is needed.

LOVE BITE MENU

- Love Bite Oysters Rockefeller

Jacques Recommends

1 chilled bottle of Woodbury's top of the line
Champagne – Brut Champagne is a 100%
Chardonnay bottle-fermented Champagne.
It is dry with hints of oak, nice fruit and bubbles.

Ingredients

*If Aromantic
Seasonings of
Seduction is
not available
in your area,
you may use
Old Bay®
Seasoning.

12 shucked oysters, drained on paper towel
12 half oyster button shells scrubbed and
    patted dry
2 lb. rock salt
4 oz. frozen chopped spinach
1 lemon
3 tablespoons chopped fresh cilantro
2 tablespoons minced green bell pepper
1 tablespoon chopped fresh basil
1 teaspoon Spicy Aromantic Seasonings of
Seduction*
¼ teaspoon fresh ground black pepper
Pinch of salt
4 tablespoons butter
¼ cup fresh cream (35%)

Preparation

Defrost spinach, press between layers of paper
towels until dry, then put aside. Melt butter in
large skillet over medium heat. Add spinach,
cilantro, basil, and bell pepper and cook until
vegetables are beginning to wilt. Add all the
seasonings and spices. Add cream and stir
constantly for 3 to 4 minutes until creamy texture.

Remove from burner. Set oven at 400º. Put rock salt in a small roasting pan and put it in oven right away. Place each oyster in each shell. Divide evenly the spinach sauce on top of each oyster. Remove pan of rock salt from oven. Press each oyster shell into the rock salt and then return to oven. Be careful, the *salt is hot*. Bake 12 minutes.

PREPARATION TIME

35 Minutes

PRESENTATION

Line a large platter with shredded lettuce. Place oysters carefully on platter. Decorate with lemon wedges and serve.

 MASTER CHEF COMMENTS

This Love Bite is the grandest creation of all!
Your companion will excel in the romance department.
Should you lick the oyster shells for an encore?

But of course!

_____

_____

_____

_____

_____

_____

_____

_____

_____

_____

_____

Love Bite No. 35
(Snowbound)

SETTING

If it is a cold, snowy night, or a cool dreary night, this Love Bite can transport you to another place. The living room in front of the fireplace or on the floor in front of the coffee table works for this Love Bite.

CREATE THE MOOD

Flowers, flowers, everywhere. The aroma from flower petals strewn over the coffee table or on the hearth of the fireplace, mixed with a few posies, bouquets or garlands will remind you of times when a young man or a woman's fancy turns to spring. Jazz or uplifting new age music can also take you to a higher plateau, leaving the dreariness behind.

LOVE BITE MENU

- Crabmeat Gratinee

Jacques Recommends

1 chilled bottle of either Dry Riesling or Reisling from Woodbury, adds wonderfully intense fruit and floral aromas to this Love Bite.

Ingredients

*If Aromantic Seasonings of Seduction is not available in your area, you may use Old Bay® Seasoning.

½ lb. lump crabmeat
¼ cup finely chopped celery
¼ cup finely chopped red bell pepper
¼ teaspoon Spicy Aromantic Seasonings of
   Seduction*
¼ teaspoon fresh ground black pepper
Pinch of salt
¼ teaspoon allspice
2 tablespoons butter
1 egg yolk
1 tablespoon flour
2 tablespoons bread crumbs
2 oz. grated Swiss cheese
¾ cup milk

Preparation

Set oven at 380°. Butter up two individual gratin dishes or custard baking dishes. With your fingertips, remove all pieces of shells and cartilage from the crabmeat. Do not break lumps. Set aside. In a medium-size frying pan or skillet, melt butter over medium heat. Add celery and red bell peppers and cook 4 minutes. Stir in flour and all the spices and seasonings and cook for 2 minutes. Add milk slowly and stir. Add breadcrumbs and stir until sauce is thickened. Add beaten egg yolk and cook 1 minute. Remove from burner and gently add crabmeat to the mixture. Fold in a few pieces of crabmeat at a time. Fill baking dishes with mixture. Divide Swiss cheese on top and bake in oven for 15 minutes.

PREPARATION TIME

30 Minutes

PRESENTATION

Line two dinner plates with lettuce leaves. Carefully place baking dishes in center of each plate and serve. You may wish to serve bread also but it is optional.

 MASTER CHEF COMMENTS

Keeping romance in full bloom will not only help in your romantic encounter sessions but it will also make it worthwhile. Don't you agree?

But of course!

_____

_____

_____

_____

_____

_____

_____

_____

_____

_____

_____

_____

0=DRY, 10=SWEET

WHITE WINES - Price Range $5.99 to 13.99

BARREL FERMENTED CHARDONNAY

Description: Fully ripened Chardonnay juice was fermented in new American Oak barrels and then aged for a year. The result is an elegant, woody, creamy full bodied wine.

Use: Seafood, poultry, even red meats with flavorful sauces

Dry/Sweet: 0

CHARDONNAY

Description: Aged in French Oak. Well-balanced with lemon, pear and vanilla aromas.

Use: All white meats and pasta

Dry/Sweet: 0

DRY RIESLING

Description: This wine is for those who enjoy rich full Riesling aromas and flavor without the sweetness.

Use: Chinese food

Dry/Sweet: 0

SEYVAL

Description: Aromas of spice, melon and pear with the distinctive grapefruit flavor.

Use: All lightly spiced food

Dry/Sweet: 1

Love Bites ❧ A Cookbook For Romantic Encounters

SEAPORT WHITE

Description: A blend of Chardonnay, Seyval and Cayuga. Flavorful and well-balanced.

Use: Seafood, chicken or turkey

Dry/Sweet: 2

RIESLING

Description: Another exceptional vintage. On the sweet side with intense Riesling fruit and floral aromas.

Use: Appetizers or desserts

Dry/Sweet: 4

NIAGARA

Description: Enjoy the taste and bouquet of this sweet native grape wine.

Use: Nice on a hot day

Dry/Sweet: 5

WHITE RENARD

Description: A sweet, fruity white wine blend with a distinctive grapey flavor.

Use: Snacks or desserts

Dry/Sweet: 5

BLUSH WINES - Price Range $5.99 - $6.49

SEAPORT BLUSH

Description: Similar to White Zinfandel with a delicate hue and fragrant bouquet.

Use: Ham or pork

Dry/Sweet: 3

BLUSH RENARD

Description: A sweet blush wine from a blend of Catawba, Delaware and Concord.

Use: Dessert

Dry/Sweet: 6

RED WINES - Price Range - $5.99 - $16.99

MERLOT

Description: A dry red wine aged in oak casks. Smooth and silky with hints of black cherry along with fruit finish.

Use: Steak

Dry/Sweet: 0

SEAPORT RED

Description: A soft, red wine with fruity aromas and lively finish.

Use: Pizza or pasta

Dry/Sweet: 2

Red Renard

Description: A sweet, fruity red wine with a delightful grapey flavor.

Use: Dessert

Dry/Sweet: 6

Cherry Wine

Description: A sweet red wine with a delightful cherry flavor.

Use: Dessert

Dry/Sweet: 10

SPARKLING WINES/CHAMPAGNES

Brut Champagne

Description: This is a 100% Chardonnay bottle fermented champagne. It is dry with hint of oak, nice fruit and bubbly.

Dry/Sweet: 0

Chautauqua Champagne

Description: This is a bottle fermented blend of Chardonnay, Seyval and Cayuga White. It is semi-dry and refreshing to the palette.

Dry/Sweet: 2

Riesling Champagne

Description: This bottle fermented Riesling is finished in a sweeter style. The rich Riesling fruit is balanced with lots of bubbles.

Dry/Sweet: 4

To place an order visit the website at
www.woodburyvineyards.com
E-mail: wv@woodburyvineyards.com
or Call 1-888-NYS-WINE (697-9463)

WOODBURY VINEYARDS WINE, GIFTS & MORE...

3230 South Roberts Road
Fredonia, New York 14063
Phone: 716-679-9463
Fax: 716-679-9464

Aurora Premium Outlets, Store #40
549 South Chillicothe Road, Route 43
Aurora, Ohio 44202
Phone: 330-562-4772
Fax: 330-562-4856

4141 Route 14
Dundee, New York 14837
Phone: 607-243-8925
Fax: 607-243-7837

(Toll Free Phone Number, Website Address and
E-mail Address are usable for all locations)